M000012970

The Epic Series

JAMES MORRELL

EPIC ADVICE FOR GRADUATES

Ten Things Every High School Graduate Should Know

Epic Advice for Graduates:
Ten Things Every High School Graduate Should Know
by James Morrell

To purchase copies of *Epic Advice for Graduates: Ten Things Every High
School Graduate Should Know* in large quantities at wholesale prices,
please contact Maryanna Young at maryanna@alohapublishing.com.

Cover design by: Fusion Creative Works and Marshall Nichols
Interior design by: Fusion Creative Works, www.fusioncw.com

ISBN: 978-1-612060-93-4

Published by Aloha Publishing

Printed in the United States of America

Contents

Introduction   9

James Michael Morrell: Author, Athlete,   13
Student, Graduate

David Gonzalez: Vice President, Masters Degree in   19
Physics and Computer Science, Published Poet

Walt Hampton: Author, Career Coach, Mountaineer   23
and Outdoor Adventureman, Attorney

Dr. Tim Sawyer: Radiation Oncologist, MD from the   25
University of Washington School of Medicine,
Father of Two Daughters

Melodee Parr: Friend, Role Model in Blind   29
Community, Innovative Professional

Whit Mitchell: Speaker, Executive Coach, Author   31

Terri Hughes: Executive Coach, Author, Leader   33

Patrick Kilroy: Colonel, U.S. Army (Retired)   35

Jeannie McCarthy-Jaggi: Adjunct Professor at Boise   39
State University, Dental Hygienist, Traveler

John Hardesty: Vice President of Digital Publishing   41
at BodyBuilding.com

Lee Elias: Game Operations and Content Production   43
Manager with the Peterborough Phantoms Ice
Hockey Club in the UK

Anna Henderson: Writer, Coach's Wife, Teacher, Mother   47

Brian M. Shirley: BSEE Stanford, Vice President of   49
Memory Solutions at Micron Technology

John Heffner: CEO of Drybar, Former President of OPI,   51
Recipient of the "City of Hope, Spirit of Life Award"
in 2007

Joel Lund: Author, Recreational Endurance Athlete,   53
Award Winning Financial Planner, Business Owner

Dr. Angela Young: Chiropractor, Yoga Instructor,   55
Nutrition Expert, Author

Bill Burns: Deacon for the Roman   59
Catholic Diocese of Boise

Kevin & Stephanie Mullani: Founders and Owners   61
of Tru Publishing

Stacy Ennis: Writer, Traveler, Speaker   63

Mark Jaszkowski: U.S. Navy officer for 23 years,   67
Master's Degree in National Resource Strategy,
Director of Development for Bishop Kelly
High School

Hannah Cross: C-Level Executive During Her College   71
Years, Editor, Blogger, Sports Enthusiast

Charley Scott: Graduated from Harvard Law School,   73
Worked for Department of Justice, Currently
Practicing Law in New York City

Jacob Barrett: Author, Blogger, Communications   75
Assistant at International Justice Mission

Justin Foster: Brand Specialist, Speaker,   77
Author, Consultant

Clifford Morton: Served in U.S. Army, International   79
Business Leader, Father, Grandfather,
Married 56 years

Bob Faw: Author, Innovator, Positive Change   81
Consultant, Speaker

Kim Foster: Editor, Friend, Wife to Award Winning   85
Teacher Chuck Foster

Terry Heffner: Dad, former Student-Athlete at Boise   89
State University, Business Owner, Life Director
with Building Contractors Association

Kurt Koontz: Author, Speaker, Traveler,   91
Recreational Elite Athlete

Matt Payn: Mentor, Dad of Two Sons, and Account   93
Executive with Global Energy & Lighting

Tobe Brockner: Entrepreneur, Author,   97
Consultant, Speaker

Scott & Maribel Morrell: Dentists & Proud Parents   99

Conclusion   103

Top Ten Most Important Things to Remember   105

Acknowledgments   113

About the Author   115

Introduction

Congratulations on your new phase of life as you graduate. At the time of the writing of this book, I was just weeks from my graduation from Bishop Kelly High School in Boise, Idaho. I am a curious person who has always had interest in stepping outside of the box and trying new things. In my lifetime, I have consistently been involved in various leadership roles like student government, athletic team captains, and campus ministry life environment.

Gathering the advice for this book was a way of helping myself and others gain knowledge from those who have learned life lessons that they want to share. Utilizing these pieces of advice will help to save all of us stress and help us reach our potential. My objective is to lead other people to accomplish things that, initially, they had no idea they could. Many of the lessons that I have learned on this topic have come from coaches, clergy, parents, and friends that I have been fortunate enough to have spent time with in my life.

Their experiences and perspectives have motivated me to compile this book.

You will value this book for your lifetime because:

1. Those who have more experience typically give the best advice. Learning from those who have lived a few more years than we have can save us a lot of time and stress by not having to "reinvent the wheel."

2. Looking to others and learning from the hard-won wisdom and insight will help you avoid making troublesome mistakes and hopefully inspire you to work hard and reach your goals.

3. As you include these pieces of advice in your daily life, you will find that you are going to be much happier and far more successful than you might have been without them.

4. Even some of the most successful people have regrets and wish they had done something different, or taken advantage of an opportunity. Seize the opportunity and apply the epic advice.

From doctors, to businessmen and women, military members, and recent graduates, this book provides a unique set of ideas, and each piece of advice comes from a different perspective. You might even start asking your friends and mentors to write their own Top Ten list or, better yet, write your own list as your commitment to staying with what you value as you move on into a new environment.

Thank you, and congratulations on taking the initiative necessary for you to make the most of your opportunities in the future. I know that you will learn as much from reading this book as I have in writing it.

Your fellow graduate,

TOP TEN THINGS EVERY GRADUATE SHOULD KNOW

10

James Michael Morrell

AUTHOR, ATHLETE, STUDENT, GRADUATE

(1.) **Get Outside of Your Comfort Zone:** Whether it be in the classroom, on the field, or in a new workplace, it is essential that you challenge yourself to grow as an individual. One of my life sayings is, "In order to be comfortable, you must leave your comfort zone." Leaving your comfort zone allows for personal development and expanded confidence. The more effort you put into getting out of your comfort zone, the more opportunities for success in future endeavors will increase.

(2.) **Fully Engage Yourself In Everything You Do:** The concept of *Be Here Now* was made famous by renowned college football coach, Chris Petersen. It embodies the idea of being in the moment and completely present in whatever you are doing at that time. If you are in class, focus completely on your studies and academic goals. If you are at a sports practice, focus all of your attention on your practice time there. If you are at a social gathering, devote all of your attention to connecting with people and expanding your relationships. Be present in the moment to achieve more than you could if you were diverting your focus.

3. **Build Your Connections:** The more people you know, the better off you will be. You never know where a small connection could lead in your future. You should be challenging yourself to meet people and establish new relationships all of the time. Don't seclude yourself to a small group of people. Force yourself to talk to people with whom you usually wouldn't associate. If you tend to spend time with one specific group of people, challenge yourself to branch out and establish a connection with anyone and everyone you can. Being part of a large network of people will pay off in the long run.

4. **Surround Yourself With Good People:** It has been commonly said that you will become the sum of the five people you spend the most time with, both in the present and over the course of a lifetime. If you are constantly surrounded by people who are a bad influence on your life, you will end up letting them sway you in directions you might have not gone otherwise. Spend time with people who have the lifestyle, career aspirations, behavior, moral standards, and a love of life that inspires you and raises the bar, affecting your own expectations and aspirations.

5. **Make An Effort To Be Respectful To Everyone:** Put effort into being an authentic person who treats others with respect. This doesn't mean you have to pursue friendships with everyone you meet. That's not realistic or genuine. Recognize that everyone comes from different backgrounds and perspectives.

Individuals raised in other countries can have similar values; however, their cultural habits and outlooks on friendships, academics, and the world are likely to be different from yours. You will make a great deal of headway in life if you recognize that differences in people are what allow teams to win, organizations to thrive, and friendships to be worth having. You never know where you might find your next best friend, business associate, or someone who may change the course of your life.

6. **Be Resilient In The Face of Adversity:** We all fail at things. It is a natural part of life and there is no way around it. Failure does not define you, however, your response to it does. Fight on in moments of little hope and use failure as a way to propel yourself forward. Our true character is shown through our actions when we are facing adversity, not success.

7. **Say "Yes" To Life:** My wrestling coach, Chad Blue, shared this concept when he was trying to convince me to join the wrestling team (something I did not want to do at the time). Although wrestling was not very appealing at first, I found that I grew as a person through learning the sport and becoming more involved in a whole new community. Don't be afraid to try new things. You will eventually find that you benefited from trying something that you were initially skeptical about.

8. **Don't Allow Others to Determine Your Success:** The more success that you have, the more likely you are to create jealousy amongst your peers. Do not allow people to bring you down just because you are taking

initiative in life and progressing towards achieve-ment. You have the capacity to determine whether or not you will reach your goals. Do not allow others to tell you how far you can go. That is up to you.

9. **Discover Yourself:** You will never be able to reach your potential if you don't challenge yourself to find out what you are really capable of becoming or achieving. So many people allow their opportunities to slip away because they never challenge themselves enough to find out what they are capable of doing. I encourage you to not hold back. Challenge yourself to discover your talents and then share them with the world. Doing this will allow you to utilize your talents to the best of your ability.

10. **Don't Over Worry About Your Future; Just Be Very Aware Of It:** It is very important for you to be con-cerned about your future and where you are going in life, but at the same time, it is essential that you take things one step at a time. Focus on your small and in-dividual priorities. Devote your attention to what you have and how you could use it to your advantage. If you spend too much time worrying about what *could* go wrong, you will eventually find that what you were worrying about *did* go wrong.

Author's Additional Advice:

11. **Have No Regrets:** Mark Twain once said, "Twenty years from now you will be more disappointed by the things that you didn't do than by the ones you did do." As humans, we naturally hold ourselves back. Only so many opportunities will present themselves, and it is

crucial for you to take advantage of every situation you can. Live your life so you can look back knowing that you did everything you could have to be content with yourself, have satisfying relationships, and use your God-given talent to make a difference in the world.

James Morrell attended Bishop Kelly High School in Boise, Idaho, where he cultivated a passion for sports, fitness, and personal development. He has been involved in youth coaching, student government, athletic team leadership, and has served as a motivational speaker. He will be enrolling at the University of Idaho in the fall of 2014 to study Business Management and Finance. James enjoys working out, playing the guitar, spending time with friends and family, and enjoying the outdoors of his home in beautiful Boise, Idaho.

10

David Gonzalez

VICE PRESIDENT, MASTERS DEGREE IN
PHYSICS AND COMPUTER SCIENCE,
PUBLISHED POET

1. Be fearless. Whether it's fear of looking stupid, or fear of failure, or fear of the unknown, it's all fear and it keeps you from the bountiful rewards awaiting you. The regret that comes with not doing something because you are afraid weighs much more heavily than doing the wrong thing.

2. Travel internationally. Perspectives, values, priorities, and reference points are all narrowly defined from the comfort of your home life. Traveling anywhere, but especially abroad, expands all of these and improves your ability to relate to different people, cultures, and situations. The memories you get to keep from travel make for terrific stories throughout your lifetime.

3. Play intramurals. There is medically documented evidence that strenuous physical activity relieves stress, exactly the kind of stress that accumulates in college. The bonds made competing together on a sports team with friends are everlasting.

(4.) Get to know your professors. Professors are people too, and generally people of a very interesting sort with unique perspectives and stories to tell. If mere intrigue isn't enough reason for you, consider the selfish reasons. Professors can help you in their class while you're taking it. Additionally, there are many things you may wish to do in your college years and beyond that require recommendations. Relationships with professors who know you and can write meaningful recommendations are invaluable.

(5.) Practice thoughtfulness. It's a lost art, though more endearing than you can imagine. A handwritten thank you note after somebody helps you, dropping whatever you're doing and rushing to lend an ear without being asked, listening intently to a friend who's spread too thin and filling their gas tank or doing their laundry – all examples of simple things that take very little time, effort, or dollars but will repay you manyfold in endearment.

(6.) Dream big. Peaks and valleys abound in life. Dreams help sustain during those valleys, and big dreams sustain for a lifetime of valleys. Always have two to three big, impossible dreams in your mind so you can get out of a slump when it's needed. When you make one of your dreams come true – which you inevitably will if you do it right – slot a new one into the mix.

(7.) Write. Write a journal. Keep a notebook of stories, or phrases, or thoughts, or theories. Maintain a blog. Write a book. The form doesn't matter nor does whether or not anyone else reads your writing, just the act of writing matters. Two things happen when you write: ideas crystalize and problems shrink. Getting a problem out of your head and into words removes the resonating and amplifying and reduces the problem to its actual size which is usually smaller than you thought.

8. Savor something deeply, for a long time, and then achieve it. The satisfaction of finally obtaining something you've savored for a long, long time fits on no scale known to man or woman. It's a combination of the deep longing and the satisfaction from the steps you executed to achieve the thing that creates such apocalyptic joy.

9. Accept friends and family for the long haul. Criticizing is easy. Finding fault is easy. Anybody can do those things. You and your friends and family will be different tomorrow, perhaps not what you were expecting or remembered. Accept them even more as a tribute to the shared time you have poured into your years together.

10. Love. One day in the very distant future you will reflect – maybe even write -- about your long and storied past. Like a topographic map, there will be Everests and Death Valleys strewn throughout. There will also be long, sustained, Rocky Mountain-like as well as Mariana Trench-like ranges. These are love. Love defines your map with geology that endures. Love matters and defines you.

David Gonzalez is a computer physicist who is currently the Vice President at Inovus Solar. He has over 25 years of experience in solution design and development. Before Inovus Solar,

David worked a 16-year career at Microsoft Corporation spanning all technical roles across the industry. He has a Bachelors Degree in Physics and Computer Science from the University of Puget Sound and a Masters Degree in Physics from Cornell University. Some of David's accomplishments include being granted six U.S. Patents, along with being a published poet. He enjoys spending time with his wife and three fiercely intelligent, humorous, and engaged children.

TOP TEN THINGS EVERY GRADUATE SHOULD KNOW

10

Walt Hampton

AUTHOR, CAREER COACH, MOUNTAINEER AND OUTDOOR ADVENTUREMAN, ATTORNEY

1. Success is a choice.

2. Excellence is a choice.

3. Our decisions shape our destiny, and we get to decide.

4. Worry is a waste.

5. Our dreams are the call of our Spirit within; we need to follow our dreams.

6. Being kind matters more than being right.

7. We make up stories about our lives; we might as well make up good ones.

8. Goals are important, but the journey and who you become along the way are what matter most.

9. Listen to your heart. Follow your heart; it always knows the way.

10. Failure is just a lesson. In every moment we get to begin again.

*Walt Hampton, J.D. is a career and success coach, speaker, and adventure photographer. He is a high altitude mountaineer, a blue water sailor, and an ultra-distance runner. He is an internationally acclaimed motivational speaker and the best-selling author of **Journeys on the Edge: Living a Life That Matters.***

TOP TEN THINGS EVERY GRADUATE SHOULD KNOW

10

Dr. Tim Sawyer

RADIATION ONCOLOGIST, MD FROM THE UNIVERSITY OF WASHINGTON SCHOOL OF MEDICINE, FATHER OF TWO DAUGHTERS

1. Once you leave high school, you meet new friends, and comparing yourself to your high school class-mates becomes meaningless. Do what's right for you, and at your own pace. Don't go to college until you know why you are going. It's okay to work for a while first if you haven't figured it out.

2. Avoid educational debt whenever possible. Significant debt can be like a ball and chain around your ankle for many years as you decide what career you want to pursue, where you want to live, and what life you want to lead.

3. Don't use college simply as a way to delay adulthood for four more years. If you have spare time in college, take extra classes that might enhance your career, get a part-time job or internship in your field of interest, or start a business and learn how to run it. You'll be glad you did.

4. At least some of your college professors will tell you that God is a myth. There are, however, many things

that science alone cannot explain. A world without God, on which rules and laws and order are based on nothing and constantly change, will become chaotic. A life without God is much less meaningful.

5. Think first. One stupid, spontaneous move can seriously and permanently impact future graduate school chances, employment opportunities, and other important long-term goals.

As you enter college, classmates will probably tell you about the stupid things you might do while drunk or high. What they probably won't explain to you is the small but meaningful percentage of your friends, family, and associates who start drinking in high school or college and appear to handle their alcohol or drugs just fine, but end up addicted, and, who, over a 20-40 year period, see their friendships, marriages, families, careers, health, happiness, and lives insidiously and relentlessly destroyed by alcohol or drugs.

6. You will see people get ahead by cutting corners and cheating. Always, *always* be honest, and always, *always* be fair. In the short term, this approach may cause you to lose some battles. In the long term, you will come out ahead.

7. Whom you marry will be the most important decision you will ever make. Choose wrongly, and happiness will be elusive.

8. Learn about money...NOW. Decisions you make in your twenties and even late teens will greatly impact your ability to live the life you want to live decades

later. Read the book, *The Millionaire Next Door*. Even if you don't agree with it, understand its point of view.

Understand the concept of exponential growth, and put money away early. Einstein said, *"Compound interest is the eighth wonder of the world. He who understands it, earns it ... he who doesn't ... pays it."*

The pursuit of shiny objects and extravagant experiences makes life much more complicated, and contrary to popular opinion, often *less* enjoyable. A lifestyle based on spending money to impress others can, like debt, become like a ball and chain around your ankle – and it just might suggest that you still haven't grasped the meaning of Einstein's quote.

9.) The saying "money can't buy happiness" is only half true. Money can enhance happiness when it is used to pursue peace of mind, freedom, and security. One inappropriately-leveraged or poorly-timed investment decision can instantly destroy a lifetime of saving and investing. Understand that if you lose 50% of your money, you have to earn 100% on what's left just to become whole again.

10.) Before you buy your dream house, consider what your dream life would be. The former might get in the way of the latter.

Finally ...

It doesn't have to take imminent death to figure life out. After Steve Jobs was diagnosed with cancer, he said: *"Your time is limited, so don't waste it living someone else's life.*

Almost everything – all external expectations, all pride, all fear of embarrassment or failure – these things just fall away in the face of death, leaving only what is truly important."

Dr. Timothy Sawyer is a radiation oncologist who currently works at the Mountain States Tumor Institute in Boise, Idaho. Dr. Sawyer graduated with an MD from the University of Washington School of Medicine in 1991, and completed his residency training in radiation oncology at the Mayo Clinic in 1996. He is actively involved in image quantification research to guide cancer treatment. Dr. Sawyer enjoys reading, spending time with his wife and two daughters, and being involved in many mountain sports near his home in Boise.

10

Melodee Parr

FRIEND, ROLE MODEL IN BLIND COMMUNITY, INNOVATIVE PROFESSIONAL

1. As much as possible, live your life so that you have no regrets.

2. The only thing worry will ever change is you, and not for the better.

3. There is good in every day. Some days you will have to look harder than others, but if you're willing to look, you will find it.

4. There will be times in life when you succeed and other times when you fail. When you succeed, great. When you fail, do it with a bang.

5. "What if" and "if only" are tyrants. Don't let your life be ruled by them.

6. When you don't know what to do, just do the next thing: put one foot in front of the other, give it a go, do your best, and see what happens.

7. Celebrate, enjoy, smile, and laugh at the little things.

8. Big or small, every choice and decision you make in life will affect someone else.

9. Your spouse, children, family, and friends are people to love, not projects to fix.

10. It really is okay to sit in quiet and peace and do nothing sometimes.

Melodee Parr is a remarkable person, as noted by the hundreds of friends around her. She has lived more than twenty five years as a blind person who inspires people to live extraordinary lives. She has been an administrative assistant, receptionist, mentor, and a person always available to pray with others since she went blind at age 18. Melodee (Roberts) Parr has been married to Mike for 18 years and they live in Meridian, Idaho.

TOP TEN THINGS EVERY GRADUATE SHOULD KNOW 10

Whit Mitchell

SPEAKER, EXECUTIVE COACH, AUTHOR

1. Ask more questions.

2. Take more risks than you think you should.

3. Travel the world, starting in New Zealand.

4. Develop confidence in yourself and what you offer the world.

5. Spend time helping the less advantaged people of the world; your life will be richer for it. Plus, you will always know friendship at its finest.

6. Start saving money the minute you graduate even if it's just $10 a week. Meet and interview financial planners right now to show you the importance of saving and managing money.

7. Listen to your parents. They have a depth of experience you don't have.

8. Take other risks such as:
   Train and Run a Marathon or some other physical challenge.

Fall deeply in love.

Apply for a job that you don't think you will get.

Really, really listen to people from all walks of life.

Talk to your parents about the challenges you are facing in your first years of college and your first years on the job.

Say (please) and (thank you) more often.

Take yourself out of the center and put others there.

Volunteer your time.

Make people with those you may have discounted their worth.

9. While in college:

Join a club or take a course you wouldn't normally take.

Challenge professors but also go for extra help.

Call and write letters to your parents and siblings.

Get uncomfortable.

10. Find what you love and dive in with reckless abandon.

Whit Mitchell is an executive coach, facilitator, and team builder. He has more than 18 years of experience as a professional coach and is a certified professional behaviors and values analyst. Whit's clients have included Fortune 500 companies such as Kodak, Bose, and United Airlines, and executive development programs at Tuck School of Business, Harvard, and Columbia University.

TOP TEN THINGS EVERY GRADUATE SHOULD KNOW

10

Terri Hughes

EXECUTIVE COACH, AUTHOR, LEADER

1. Don't be afraid to try things or take risks that may feel uncomfortable. For example, I regret shying away from courses in college or certain jobs because I was afraid I wouldn't do well.

2. Stay curious about everything. It will keep you interesting and young and help you understand your own strengths!

3. Be good to yourself and accept where you are (without comparing yourself to others). Remember you are a work in progress, so enjoy the journey!

4. Learn to laugh at yourself along the way. You will create great stories throughout your lifetime.

5. Keep a journal and record your thoughts and feelings. You'll be surprised at how helpful this can be – both in the writing and reviewing – to help you get to know who you are and who you are becoming.

6. Spend at least two hours a day without any electronic devices (i.e. when you are taking a walk or a bike ride, just enjoy the sounds around you).

7. Even though school may be out, never stop learning and challenging yourself to improve.

8. Take advantage of every opportunity, even the part-time job that isn't your career choice. You will likely learn valuable skills that will serve you well in the future.

9. Don't take life or yourself too seriously. Try not to worry about things outside of your control, and know that how you decide to see things is the only real control you have.

10. Find a nonprofit organization that inspires you and volunteer to help. You'll be amazed at how good it will make you feel.

Terri Hughes is a leadership coach and author of **Simple Shifts: Effective Leadership Changes Everything***. Terri works with leaders across a wide array of industries. Over the years she has learned that there is a simple catalyst for effective leadership and personal development: self-awareness.*

TOP TEN THINGS EVERY GRADUATE SHOULD KNOW **10**

Patrick J. Kilroy

COLONEL, U.S. ARMY (RETIRED)

1. Your two most important qualities are character and integrity. Both take years to build; both can be irreparably damaged in a few regrettable moments. No one can take them away from you; they are yours to keep. Guard and protect them jealously.

2. Keep your grandparents, parents, role-models, mentors, teachers, and coaches engaged in some small way in your life. They helped you get where you are and can help you get where you're aiming to go. One of your greatest gifts, and their sublime joys, is your telling them so.

3. Strive to be a gentleman/woman. Chivalry is neither obsolete nor dead nor quaintly archaic. Build your professional reputation and network upon your good works. Respect others and be polite. What goes around comes around.

4. Find people who will give you unvarnished feedback. Then, thank them when they do. Remember peers

who helped you along the way. In return, help them succeed. Recommend a peer for an award and public recognition. Cheer loudly from the front row when it happens.

5. In some small way, serve your local community. Make it a point to "pay forward" a good turn you've not necessarily earned but received nonetheless. Encourage your friends to do the same. This is a score worth keeping.

6. Pay your own way as best as you can. Pay attention to your money and live within your means. Whether you have a lot or a little, watch it and be deliberate with it. Pay cash for everything – especially shiny things.

7. Get out and enjoy life away from your iPhone and Xbox. Technology can be a trap or crutch that's sometimes confused for competence. Don't allow yourself to be misled by the allure of gadgetry. People and relationships are what really matter.

8. Be a "go-to" guy/gal known for delivering the job done right. Do the right thing, especially when no one is watching. Inwardly celebrate when you've been called upon, held accountable, and achieved something meaningful.

9. Keep a journal. Note your life's unique experiences—whether good or bad, memorable or forgettable. Be familiar with current events and strive to understand history and its connection to important contemporary issues. Seek personal growth.

10. Live life looking forward with no regrets. Mistakes build character and resilience. Learn from the past, but don't live in it.

A retired career military officer now in business, Pat is a 1986 graduate of the U.S. Military Academy at West Point and earned graduate degrees from the U.S. Naval War College, the NATO Defense College and Boise State University. Pat's most treasured accomplishments are having been married and being ever in love with Monique — his wife of 27 years — and their having raised together three highly successful and amazing children: John, Allie, and Madelaine. The Kilroy family lives in Boise, Idaho.

TOP TEN THINGS EVERY GRADUATE SHOULD KNOW

10

Jeannie McCarthy-Jaggi

ADJUNCT PROFESSOR AT BOISE STATE UNIVERSITY, DENTAL HYGIENIST, TRAVELER

1. Truly educated people never graduate.

2. Change challenges us to simultaneously let go and take on. It reminds us that life is a journey of constant creation.

3. The key to life is adaptation.

4. Seek to form your own opinions; do not keep recycling ones given to you by others.

5. Read, read, read: textbooks, novels, newspapers. Keep feeding your knowledge base.

6. Cultivate and cherish good friends. Do not isolate yourself because life is always happier when shared with people you care about.

7. Become the parent you wished you'd had. Become the boss you'd like to have. Become the teacher you wish you'd had. Become the spouse you would like to have, etc.

8.) Be grateful. Do not take the comforts of your life for granted. Each day, take a moment to find a glimpse of The Garden of Eden in your life – even if it is "just" having a pillow beneath your head.

9.) Show up for class. The act of showing up and listening, no matter how difficult the class might be, usually makes a whole letter grade of difference.

10.) Albert Einstein once said, "Imagination is more important than knowledge." Exercise and feed your creativity and imagination. It is imagination fueled by knowledge that finds cures.

Jeannie McCarthy-Jaggi is a dental hygienist and adjunct professor at Boise State University. She has practiced dental hygiene in both the United States and Switzerland, enjoying the clinical aspects of her work and the enrichment of working with people from different cultures. A great believer in world travel, language acquisition, and lifelong learning, Jeannie has redirected her career to teaching, mentoring students, and working on Health Science research. Jeannie enjoys outdoor exercise, travel, and spending time with family and friends.

TOP TEN THINGS EVERY GRADUATE SHOULD KNOW

10

John Hardesty

VICE PRESIDENT OF DIGITAL PUBLISHING AT BODYBUILDING.COM

1. Don't settle for anything less than what you have pictured for your life.

2. Find your passion and purpose. You should love your career and find meaning in it.

3. Stay physically fit and invest in your body. It's the first impression for your work ethic, commitment, and ability to succeed.

4. Find mentors and role models. Surround yourself with successful people.

5. Work hard; play hard. Find the right balance early on in your life.

6. Don't just follow the curriculum that's been built for everyone before you. Tweak and adjust to fit your vision and skills.

7. Spend quality time with family and friends. They are your best support group through the good times and the bad.

8. Participate in internship programs while finding your career path. You'll learn things you can't learn from a book.

9. Identify your strengths and weaknesses. Refine your strengths constantly. Align with people that make up for your weaknesses.

10. Take advantage of your youth. You're young, creative, motivated, and on the cutting-edge. Take risks now, make mistakes quickly, and learn from them!

John Hardesty is currently the Vice President of Digital Publishing at Bodybuilding.com, the world's largest online health and fitness website. John received a Bachelors of Fine Arts in Graphic Design at Boise State University and used his passion for branding to start his first advertising agency when he was 22 years old. John currently resides in Boise, Idaho.

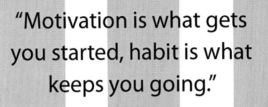

"Motivation is what gets you started, habit is what keeps you going."

—Jim Ryan

TOP TEN THINGS EVERY GRADUATE SHOULD KNOW

10

Lee Elias

GAME OPERATIONS AND CONTENT PRODUCTION MANAGER WITH THE PETERBOROUGH PHANTOMS ICE HOCKEY CLUB IN THE UK

1. Mess Up. Don't be afraid to fail. Very few are blessed to know what they want to do when they graduate high school, so use the next few years as time to mess up and fall down and try again. Find what you want to do because "the rest of your life" is a very long time.

2. Work. Get a jump-start on the rest of your peers by getting some work experience over the next few years. Degrees are nice but nothing is more attractive to employers than experience.

3. Get in the habit of introducing yourself to people whether it is a college professor or a new person you are working with. Giving people a name to go with a face can go a long way.

4. Don't be afraid to follow your dreams. People don't have to support your dream but should support your right to HAVE a dream.

5. When chasing down a dream, don't forget to embrace the journey regardless of whether or not you accomplish your goal.

6. Think before you post things online; the digital realm is eternal. The "funny picture from last night" may come to haunt you years from now.

7. Base all your relationships (friends, partners, colleagues, etc.) on trust. If there is no trust, what's the point?

8. You will have one or two real, lifelong "friends" in your life if you are lucky. Make sure you choose them wisely and pray they did the same.

9. Learn to love yourself before "falling in love" with others. You can't give someone something you don't have.

10. Gain experience through others. You don't always have to experience things yourself to learn a lesson.

Lee currently holds the position of Game Operations and Content Production Manager with the Peterborough Phantoms Ice Hockey Club who are based in England. Some of his professional work experience includes having held positions at the National Hockey League, Madison Square Garden, NBC Sports, A&E Television Networks, and Hearst Media Services. He is a graduate of Drexel University's Sports Management Masters program at the institution's Goodwin School of Professional Studies.

TOP TEN THINGS EVERY GRADUATE SHOULD KNOW

Anna Henderson

WRITER, COACH'S WIFE, TEACHER, MOTHER

1. Don't lose sight of your true passion or calling in life. It is easy to compromise your dream career for a job that simply pays the bills.

2. Don't be afraid to ask questions. This can save you a ton of possible time, money, or embarrassment.

3. Don't maintain friendships that drain you. If you are having to work to enjoy someone's company, it is time to move on.

4. Don't hide who you really are. Not being true to yourself is the worst form of betrayal.

5. Don't choose social media over a good night's sleep. Studies show that a lack of quality sleep can lead to poor concentration and memory, and, in many cases, weight gain.

6. Do consider the other side before you judge or speak out against something or someone. A healthy argument is a great way to learn new things.

(7.) Do commit to eating a balanced diet and getting exercise at least five days a week. Your metabolism will change as you get older. Counter a slow metabolism with whole foods, lean proteins, water, and regular physical activity. Watch out for excess sugar; it is linked to many health problems.

(8.) Do keep playing outside, like you did in elementary school. Two cheap anti-depressants are moderate doses of sunlight (vitamin D) and good, old-fashioned FUN.

(9.) Do travel as much as you can. Adults have a way of eventually becoming more "anchored," making exploring new places more challenging.

(10.) Do learn to manage your money. Educate yourself, as soon as possible, on wise ways to stay out of debt and save money. Be very careful with credit cards.

Anna Henderson worked approximately fifteen years in Texas public schools, teaching a range of children from 2nd grade to seniors in high school. She is currently working to raise her two daughters, Maddie and Sophie, and support her basketball coaching husband, Danny. Anna also spends time on her passion: writing. She just recently moved to Boise, Idaho, which she has fallen in love with, despite her strong Texas roots and loyalty.

TOP TEN THINGS EVERY GRADUATE SHOULD KNOW 10

Brian M. Shirley

BSEE STANFORD,
VICE PRESIDENT OF MEMORY SOLUTIONS
AT MICRON TECHNOLOGY

1. In college, push yourself to try as many new things as possible: new classes, sports, hobbies, musical instruments, whatever. You will never again be surrounded by such diversity. It's as easy as it will ever be to jump in, and you can sleep when you're dead.

2. Truly get to know as many people as possible. Be happy to see them, show interest in them, and find out what animates them. You'll never regret it.

3. Beware of scientific theories or movements that rely more on shutting down criticism and intimidation than on actually explaining the facts.

4. If the party scene is your thing, stick with beer, avoid hard alcohol, and for gosh sakes, don't ever drink and drive.

5. In college, you will be surrounded with people who see massive wealth redistribution as the answer. It doesn't work, and it's never worked. No sane person would waste their time and capital building new job-

creating businesses if they knew they were just going to get knee-capped when they succeeded.

(6.) In your core freshman classes, read the darn books and go to all of the early lectures. It's worth it.

(7.) Ease up on everyone and try to empathize. Most people are fighting some sort of internal battle, be it large or small.

(8.) If you like where you work (or just like the paycheck), make yourself indispensable. Get in early and stay late. Think big, solve problems, make things happen, and don't whine. It's work ethic coupled with ambition. You will separate yourself from the herd quickly.

(9.) Don't ever speed when driving through a neighborhood.

(10.) Life is clumpy. It just is. Sometimes that's good, sometimes bad, but if the dice are hot, stay at that table.

Brian Shirley lives in Boise, Idaho, and is the Vice President of Memory Solutions at Micron Technology. Before Micron, he attended Stanford University and earned a BS in electrical engineering. Brian has been married to his wife, Linda, for nearly 19 years and together have proudly raised two sons, Zane and Luke. Aside from Micron, Brian has served on the board of Concordia Law School, Boise Art Museum and the College of Idaho. He enjoys spending his free time mountain biking and enjoying the scenery around the state.

TOP TEN THINGS EVERY GRADUATE SHOULD KNOW

10

John Heffner

CEO OF DRYBAR, FORMER PRESIDENT OF OPI, RECIPIENT OF THE "CITY OF HOPE, SPIRIT OF LIFE AWARD" IN 2007

1. Don't be in such a hurry. Enjoy your life *now*. There is plenty of time ahead.

2. Kindness always wins...always.

3. Look for the person in the room who is alone or out of place and put them at ease. You just might make a friend.

4. Don't run with the crowd. Instead, lead the crowd.

5. If you are in a rut, pick yourself up and climb out. The world is waiting for you.

6. Drugs are not cool. I've never taken one and haven't missed a thing.

7. You *always* have more options than you think...so think.

8. Don't wait for the right moment. It may never come. Just do it.

9. *Always* act with integrity in business...and in life.

10. If you want to be happily married, marry a happy person.

John Heffner, CEO of Drybar, a nation's largest chain of blow-out salons, was also President of global cosmetics power brand OPI, as well as executive positions in Unilever and Procter & Gamble. John is also Chairman emeritus of the Professional Beauty Association and Chairman of the San Diego Chapter of YPO (Young Presidents Organization). His greatest accomplishment is his 23 year marriage to his wife Kristine and raising two wonderful sons, Andrew and Christopher.

TOP TEN THINGS EVERY GRADUATE SHOULD KNOW

Joel Lund

AUTHOR, RECREATIONAL ENDURANCE ATHLETE, AWARD WINNING FINANCIAL PLANNER, BUSINESS OWNER

1. Don't just follow your dreams. Chase them like the T1000 Terminator. Be relentless and dare greatly.

2. No one owes you anything that you won't give yourself. If opportunities aren't coming your way, then make your own. Be inventive. Create. Inspire.

3. Embrace the responsibility that comes with living your life fully. Then help others do the same.

4. Say "please" and "thank you" every chance you get. In fact, make up reasons to say them.

5. Take care of yourself. You're fragile and finite, and the world needs your uniqueness.

6. Learn to listen well—really well. It's hard to do, so start learning the skill early. Then practice, all the time.

7. Be compassionate. The world is tough enough already. Respect others, even when it's tough. Your turn will come.

8.) Lead. Lead now. The world needs great leaders. Why not you? Why not now? Don't wait until you're "grown up."

9.) Take risks and do something every day that scares you a little. Get comfortable with being uncomfortable. You'll do great things and surprise yourself along the way.

10.) With everything you have—all of your energy, focus and determination—strive to make the world better than you find it. Becoming famous is not worthy of your efforts. Making a difference is.

Joel Lund is an introvert, comfortable with being uncomfortable. Enough so that he has been on stage countless times, one time in front of more than 2,000 people. Though not an athlete, he's completed the Seattle-to-Portland Bicycle Classic, riding 200 miles in two days (once on a tandem) as well as completed a 5.11 climb in Joshua Tree. His leadership in the financial services industry was honored, internationally, through the worst years of the Great Recession. He cherishes the accomplishments of becoming an author him are in both non-fiction and fiction and inspiring his teenage daughter to become a great author. His current focus is to build an exceptional business focused on to inspiring people, along with his wife, Janet.

TOP TEN THINGS EVERY GRADUATE SHOULD KNOW 10

Dr. Angela Young

CHIROPRACTOR, YOGA INSTRUCTOR, NUTRITION EXPERT, AUTHOR

1. Visualize and write down how you want your life to look in 5, 10, 15, 20, and 50 years. After you write it down, figure out how to create it. Your written goals give direction to your life and become much more concrete and actionable once put on paper.

2. Make and maintain as many connections as you can. Strive to make a positive memorable impression on your professors, classmates, employers, co-workers, etc. — as many people as you can. A strong network of people who know, like, and trust you is invaluable.

3. Blog and establish a tasteful social media presence. Make your online presence attractive so future employers, clients, or other professionals feel confident in your knowledge and communication skills.

4. Take care of your physical self. This is the only body you have. You can't abuse your body for years with lack of sleep, unhealthy food, and an influx of caffeine and expect to have good health as you get older.

5. Pursue the things you're passionate about instead of what others tell you that you should pursue. Realize that it takes money to live and you may have to have multiple income streams if you pursue careers with low income potential.

6. Realize there is no "right career path." People in all types of careers have rewarding and satisfying jobs. There is no perfect way to get where you want to go.

7. Realize a lack of time or money is not a good excuse to go after what you really want in your life. These are two of the most common excuses you will ever hear. Don't let these excuses rule your life.

8. Have confidence in yourself and your ability to do what you want to do and be who you want to be. People buy into the confidence you have in yourself. Confidence is an inner knowing rather than an inflated version of oneself.

9. Stay optimistic. Most young people are accused of being overly optimistic. You can accomplish much more by being optimistic and believing you can rather than by believing you can't.

10. Don't take yourself so seriously. Mistakes are rarely fatal. It is better to be out there trying to create than to get hung up on and paralyzed by the fear of making a wrong decision.

Dr. Angela Young has a practical, yet revolutionary, approach to personal health. She believes that pain and sickness shouldn't drive your decision to get healthy. She is leading a movement to support individuals with simple, effective health choices that are not driven by cultural or media myths. In her personal chiropractic practice, getting healthy and staying healthy is a partnership.

TOP TEN THINGS EVERY GRADUATE SHOULD KNOW 10

Bill Burns

DEACON FOR THE ROMAN CATHOLIC DIOCESE OF BOISE

1. Whether you have a faith in God or have no faith, always seek the truth regardless of where it will take you. Once you have found it, do not discard it for a convenient or comfortable lie.

2. Seek mentors who are people of good character. Listen to their advice and emulate their behavior.

3. Listen to your feelings, but don't let them be the sole arbiter of your decisions.

4. Be quick to forgive when you are wronged and quick to apologize when you have wronged.

5. Don't be too anxious to jettison the practices and traditions of your parents. They can often be an anchor in the stormy times of your life.

6. Always treat others with respect and dignity as people, especially those who serve you or are at your mercy.

7. Do not be afraid to fail or to take risks.

8. Always try to seek out the best in people.

9. Give credit to others when it is due. Accept credit with humility.

10. Get into the habit of serving others. In the end, a self-centered life is an unhappy, joyless life.

Bill Burns is a content-management and publishing consultant. He has master's degrees in English and Theology, black belts in two martial arts, and is a deacon for the Roman Catholic Diocese of Boise.

TOP TEN THINGS EVERY GRADUATE SHOULD KNOW 10

Kevin & Stephanie Mullani

FOUNDERS AND OWNERS OF
TRU PUBLISHING

1. Take your college transcript seriously. It really does stay with you forever. Remember, however, building relationships is as important as your grades.

2. Get comfortable with being uncomfortable. Most true growth happens just outside your comfort zone.

3. If there is a dream on your heart, pursue it. People may give well-intentioned advice to deter you from your dream, but if you do not sing the song that is on your heart you will live with regret. Focus on the kind of work you love and believe has value for the world. If you work only for money, you waste precious time. Use your gifts and the money will find its way to you.

4. Know when to have fun, and when to be serious.

5. Express gratitude. If someone does a nice thing for you, makes a connection for you, or inspires you – thank them! An attitude of gratitude goes a long way.

6. Be kind to everyone; you don't know their story.

7. Loss and frustration are part of life. Take each experience as an opportunity to grow, improve, and learn from.

8. Strive to make joy a priority in all decisions.

9. Focus only on the thoughts that you want to become reality in your life. The power of your imagination is stronger than you may realize.

10. Be open to different points of view. The biodiversity of life on earth makes for a healthy ecosystem. Likewise, biodiversity of friendships can make life healthier and richer for understanding and "seeing" life from different angles.

Kevin and Stephanie Mullani are the founders and owners of Tru Publishing and the proud parents of Wyatt and Anna. Kevin is an Air Force veteran who strives to live joyfully in the present. He is happily married to his soul-mate Stephanie, an accomplished artist and author whose clients include many Fortune 500 companies. She is also an avid adventurer, traveler, and lover of life. After living in various places around the globe, they currently reside in Idaho.

"In response to those who say to stop dreaming and face reality, I say **keep dreaming** and make reality."

—Kristian Kan

TOP TEN THINGS EVERY GRADUATE SHOULD KNOW

Stacy Ennis

WRITER, TRAVELER, SPEAKER

1. Know that, at any point in your life, you can make the decision to change. Academics, attitude, health, even success—anything can improve if you choose to aim for greatness.

2. Never say, "I can't." Instead, ask yourself, "How can I learn to do that?" or "Who can I ask for help?"

3. Don't be afraid to take risks and do things that push your limits. Some of the greatest rewards in life come from challenges that scare you.

4. Take care of your body: eat well, exercise, get plenty of sleep, and don't get too stressed out.

5. Avoid student loans at all cost. With debt, you start adulthood significantly behind.

6. Know that life has already started. It doesn't begin when you earn a high school or college diploma. Each choice you make contributes to who you are now and who you'll be in the future.

7.) Stop trying to find the right guy or girl to date. Become a person *worth* dating, and you'll attract someone who's perfect for you.

8.) Keep in mind that the greatest moments of your life should always be ahead of you.

9.) Travel! There is nothing that has such a profound impact as being exposed to new locales, experiences, and people. Travel also grows your heart.

10.) Know that you are no different from individuals who have achieved excellence. They are just ordinary people who chose to live extraordinary lives. You, too, can accomplish anything you wish. Truly.

Stacy Ennis (stacyennis.com) is a book and magazine editor, writer, and speaker, as well as the author of The Editor's Eye: A Practical Guide to Transforming Your Book from Good to Great. After spending two years abroad in the Dominican Republic and Vietnam, she moved to Boise, Idaho, where she currently lives with her husband and daughter.

TOP TEN THINGS EVERY GRADUATE SHOULD KNOW

Mark Jaszkowski

U.S. NAVY OFFICER FOR 23 YEARS, MASTER'S DEGREE IN NATIONAL RESOURCE STRATEGY, DIRECTOR OF DEVELOPMENT FOR BISHOP KELLY HIGH SCHOOL

1. Get behind the wheel. Too many people spend their life in the passenger seat looking out the windshield and watching their life unfold like a TV show. Slide over into the driver's seat and take control. There are no do-overs and a day gone by can never be replayed. If you don't like what you are seeing, turn the wheel. It isn't rocket science; you can do anything you want if you just do it.

2. Routines are harder to sustain than a flurry of action, but you'll be better rewarded if you do. In your endeavors don't create circumstances that require you to dramatically respond to every crisis that comes along. Rather, take the long view and engage in developing steady, predictable routines that prevent the crises in the first place. You will be happier and more effective if you do.

3. The importance of people. No one was ever successful by themselves, they got where they were with a lot of help. The best way to help yourself is to help others.

They will then willingly become the rungs of your career ladder.

4. It is the poor workman who blames his tools. You will rarely, if ever, have the perfect people and resources needed to accomplish what you want to achieve. Anyone can play poker with four aces in hand, but you are just as often dealt deuces. A true poker player can win with a hand full of deuces. Don't waste energy blaming the deal; learn to play with whatever hand you have. Leadership is the art of getting someone to do something to your standards.

5. There are two ways to change behavior in people, the carrot and the stick. We all seem to spend an in-ordinate amount of time on discipline and punish-ment, when praise and encouragement are generally cheaper and easier, and always more effective. Hold up those who live the desired organizational culture with praise. Take the agenda from those who might drive it elsewhere.

6. Losing control of your emotions may make you feel better, but it will more than likely detract from efforts to solve the problem. Temper is wasted energy. When problems present—as they will—remember, nothing is ever as good or as bad as it seems initially. Use a cool head and seek a solution. Enjoy drama only at the theater.

7. Equitable distribution of work is not appropriate in high functioning organizations; and neither should be equitable distribution of reward. You may work more or less than some in your organization. You may be

rewarded more or less than others. Don't focus on the unfairness you may encounter. Keep your sights on your goals and doing your best. Your efforts will pay off.

8. Your priorities establish your credibility. Your focus is an indication of your ability to see the big picture and support the organization you belong to. Focus on what is important, not on what is easy or on what you like to do. For you regarding those who report to you, remember that if you don't give people important things to do, they will make what they do important. Give them important tasks and then support them. You will both get further ahead.

9. Your good example is not always emulated, but your poor example becomes a ready excuse for others. It is much easier for people to do the wrong thing if somebody else is displaying bad behavior. Setting a good example will guide people in the right direction, while setting the wrong example will subsidize poor behavior in others.

10. Get in touch with your Creator. Regardless of your faith tradition, you need to make progress on your spiritual journey. If your spiritual life is weak, the rest of your life is likely to follow. It is also not a good idea to be your own moral compass. Regardless of how much you have, the day will come in your life when prayer is all that you have. It is nice when that time comes if you know you can call on your Creator.

Mark Jaszkowski is a native of the Pacific Northwest. He received a Bachelor's of Science in Business/Finance and Naval Science at Oregon State University. He served as a U. S. Navy officer for 23 years primarily on surface ships. He also served in the Bureau of Naval Personnel in Washington D.C., as a Communications Officer in London, and as a Maritime Operations Officer for NATO in Belgium. He holds a Master's Degree in National Resource Strategy from the National Defense University in Washington D.C. Following his military service, he paid it forward as Director of Development for Bishop Kelly High School for ten years.

TOP TEN THINGS EVERY GRADUATE SHOULD KNOW

10

Hannah Cross

C-LEVEL EXECUTIVE DURING HER COLLEGE
YEARS, EDITOR, BLOGGER, SPORTS ENTHUSIAST

(1.) Your parents are cooler and wiser than you've realized. Find things to appreciate about them.

(2.) Everything doesn't have to happen right now. A little perspective goes a long way.

(3.) Be mentored, encouraged, and kept accountable by someone who cares.

(4.) Listen with your heart, not just your ears.

(5.) Talk to little kids on a regular basis. Their life philosophy is refreshing.

(6.) Thank God for your clothes, your food, and the roof over your head. You're most likely wealthier than the majority of the world.

(7.) Do things for people who can't repay you. Genuinely serve.

(8.) Develop little things into meaningful moments. Realize a cup of coffee, a hug, or a genuine note of appreciation can make another's day.

9.) Sing old hymns. Read classic books. New isn't always better.

10.) Chase God's vision and heart. His plans for you are better than anything you could make for yourself. Twists and turns are okay.

Hannah Cross started working on where she wants to take her career by taking a job at a publishing company as an intern when she was sixteen. She began blogging the following year and taking on book size editing projects a year later when she was just 18. She traveled abroad several times before the age of 20 and loves sports, studying nutrition, helping people as well as gaining skills and work experience most people overlook until much later in life.

TOP TEN THINGS EVERY GRADUATE SHOULD KNOW 10

Charley Scott

GRADUATED FROM HARVARD LAW SCHOOL, WORKED FOR DEPARTMENT OF JUSTICE, CURRENTLY PRACTICING LAW IN NEW YORK CITY

1. You don't need to figure out your life's path right away. You will have many future opportunities to re-invent yourself, so take risks and explore the things that make you tick.

2. Although you are striking out on your own, you will always be able to go home. But don't take that for granted! Make an effort to stay close to your family and friends.

3. Be compassionate toward—and not contemptuous of—those who are going through tough times. Even if you never find yourself in their shoes, you won't enjoy looking back on times when you acted like a jerk.

4. Take good care of your teeth and your skin. This is especially important if you want to be taken seriously in the professional world.

5. Take advantage of good opportunities, even if they seem intimidating. You will regret the things you didn't do more than the things that you did do.

6. Honesty really is the best policy, so tell the truth even when it's awkward. You can always find a tactful way to tell the truth, but you can never recover from telling a lie.

7. Your taste in music will get lamer. If you find yourself saying things like, "I used to like this band, but their new stuff is too weird," the problem is probably you.

8. The older you get, the harder it will be to break your bad habits. (So start now!)

9. It's wise to keep work or studies separate from the rest of your life, but sometimes you'll be too busy to do that. Make time for people you care about, even if it's spent quietly studying together.

10. Be a self-actualizing optimist: always (especially if you're feeling down) remind yourself that the best is yet to come, then take a step—big or small—toward making it happen!

Charley Scott is an energy and environmental lawyer in New York. After receiving undergraduate and graduate degrees in Classics, he changed career paths and went to law school, clerked for a federal judge, and spent several years as an appellate litigator for the government before moving into private legal practice.

TOP TEN THINGS EVERY GRADUATE SHOULD KNOW

10

Jacob Barrett

AUTHOR, BLOGGER, COMMUNICATIONS ASSISTANT AT INTERNATIONAL JUSTICE MISSION

1. After high school, your chances of making lifelong friendships decline rapidly. For each minute you spend on making new friends, spend one on building a friendship you already have. It will benefit you more.

2. Always be thankful for your parents and the others who helped you reach your potential. Let them know how thankful you are often.

3. Embrace structure. Structure always increases productivity and quality of life.

4. Don't be afraid to change the structure. There is always room for improvement.

5. If you don't have a mentor, find one. Everyone needs a spiritual/life mentor to whom they can ask advice on anything. Leaving high school might seem like the time you want a mentor the least, but you will soon find you never needed one more.

6. Be a mentor. If you have a younger sibling or friend a few years behind you in school, open yourself up to

giving them some help along the way. Building relationships outside of your peer group will make you a more complete person.

7. Fear will always be your biggest enemy. Never stop doing the right things that you don't want to do.

8. You can have most any job if you will communicate well, work hard, and want it.

9. Don't underestimate the value of purpose. Finding a purpose in whatever you are doing will always make it more rewarding.

10. Be excited for each day. It will have new challenges, experiences, and joys.

Jacob Barrett is a 2010 high school graduate from Covenant Academy in Meridian, Idaho and a 2014 Graduate of Hillsdale College in Hillsdale, Michigan. He is serving as the Communications Assistant for the International Justice Mission, in Delhi, India, in addition to his rich life as a teaching assistant, author, blogger, and friend.

Justin Foster

BRAND SPECIALIST, SPEAKER, AUTHOR, CONSULTANT

1. Choose your friends wisely. More specifically, choose carefully who you decide to do business with: partners, clients, etc. Adopt Reagan's Cold War strategy of "trust but verify."

2. You get what you pay for. This applies to what you are paying for as well as the value you place on your talents and skills — and it includes both time and money.

3. Time is money. When you get paid for trading your time for dollars, time is your inventory. Control it carefully and invest it wisely.

4. Pride comes before fall. Ego-based decisions create expensive failures. Arrogance makes you stupid by massively increasing the number of blind spots.

5. Pressure creates diamonds. Stress is what you feel when you don't know what you are doing or you have committed to too much. Pressure is beautiful, because it means you have confidence in your ability and look forward to the pressure of expectations.

6. You can't improve what you don't measure. As you gain experience, you gain wisdom and instincts. However, adding data, measurements, and goals to instincts is where improvement and excellence comes from.

7. No pain. No gain. I've learned very little from the "wins." In fact, they tend to feed my ego. I learn every time I fail. While I don't seek failure, I do seek pain because I know it is teaching me something.

8. You only get one first impression. Manage your personal brand wisely. Be yourself, but not too much. Dress well. Speak well. Treat others well.

9. It's not what you know. It's who you know. In this era of social business, you can't have too many friends. Find the ones who fill you up and serve them. By serving their interests, you will expand your influence.

10. Success is a journey, not a destination. Stay humble. Serve others. Stay relevant. Work on your whole person — body, mind, spirit. If you are bored, you are doing it wrong.

Justin believes that being awesome is the best brand strategy. So he teaches people how to do this for themselves and their companies by helping them discover what makes them awesome and amplifying it to the right audiences. Justin's new book Human Bacon: A Man's Guide to Creating an Awesome Personal Brand is a 2014 release.

TOP TEN THINGS EVERY GRADUATE SHOULD KNOW

10

Clifford Morton

SERVED IN U.S. ARMY, INTERNATIONAL BUSINESS LEADER, FATHER, GRANDFATHER, MARRIED 56 YEARS

1. Your education is just starting. Regardless of whether you plan to go to college or straight off to work at something or emigrate to New Zealand, your education is just starting.

2. Direct yourself. It's easy and perhaps normal to say, "I don't know what I want to do." At this juncture, that's okay, but do something useful that interests you.

3. Everything around you has been invented since your Grandmother was born. Our world is in its infancy. wow! What does that offer you?

4. Live in the moment but concentrate on the future.

5. Experiment.

6. Your health, the shape you're in, your weight, etc., reflect your style. Make sure you are presenting what *you* want.

7. Consciously develop your code. What do you believe? How should you treat others? Gentleman, especially

consider how you should treat ladies, and know what's right and what's not.

8. Spend or give some time each month with old people, poor people. Don't give money; give of yourself.

9. God, Country, Family balance your life and, above all, have fun.

10. If you don't know how to accomplish the above, figure it out; but do it, don't have it happen.

Clifford Morton has over 30 years experience in banking in the USA. Having spent over 20 years with Security Pacific National Bank and later The Bank of California NA, he joined Boise Cascade Corporation, where he occupied a number of executive positions, including that of Chief Financial Officer. He founded Clifford A Morton Inc. (CAMi) in 1986, an international investment banking boutique. Mr. Morton served in U.S. President Gerald Ford's Administration as Deputy Administrator of the U.S. Small Business Administration, and as an Adjunct Professor at Stanford Business School, California. He is also the author of Managing Operations in Emerging Companies.

TOP TEN THINGS EVERY GRADUATE SHOULD KNOW

10

Bob Faw

AUTHOR, INNOVATOR, POSITIVE CHANGE CONSULTANT, SPEAKER

1. Write life goals: You can change them at any time, but it's motivating to have goals that energize you to work hard. Specific goals such as "become an architect," and vague goals such as "I want to travel a lot," help focus your decisions. (Unless your goals hurt others.)

2. Nurture your close relationships: Strong family times and friendships will help you weather the tough times and enjoy the good ones. Nurture the most important relationships like you would a flower garden. (Unless these folks hold you back, in which case, do some weeding.)

3. Competing can derail you: It's far more important to find work that helps you enjoy your life than it is to compete against others. It's possible to make a lot of stupid choices that lead you to a dead end job trying to prove something to someone else. (Unless you're going for the Olympics.)

4. Own your success: You, and you alone, are responsible for your successes in life. There are countless people

that can help, but waste no time blaming others when you don't make it. Instead, immediately focus on how to get back on track. (Unless your goal is to successfully play the blame game.)

5. Ask for help: There are so many resources available to you. Ethically use whatever it takes to help you get where you want to go. Trying to do it alone just takes longer and is less fun in the end. (Unless you truly are superhuman.)

6. Laugh a lot: Life is short and precious. Enjoy as much as you can. Make sure to laugh multiple times per day. (Unless you're in court.)

7. Create good habits: To be excellent at your future profession you'll need habits of working hard, thinking critically, and adapting to change well. (Unless you're goal is to be a lifelong participant in sleep studies.)

8. Be a contributor: One of the greatest sources of lasting fulfillment is making a positive difference in the world, especially if you're able to use your strengths to do it. (Unless your strength is plagiarism.)

9. Channel your passion: Find creative ways to get paid doing things that you truly enjoy doing. There are many jobs out there you've never heard of that involve your doing things you like to do, at least part of the time. (Unless it might end up with you in prison.)

10. Create positive credibility: Only put online what will help you achieve your life goals. Steer clear of the temptations to badmouth people, gripe about petty

stuff, and do not engage in extreme behavior. (Unless you want to become an extremist radio host.)

Bob Faw is a positive change consultant, transformational thought leader, and sought after dynamic speaker who motivates people around the world to make positive changes in their lives. Bob lives in New Hampshire with Zsuzsi Gero (his sweetheart) and Nisha (their dog). His passions include hiking, dancing, swimming, and learning the latest on brain science.

"You have brains in your head.
You have feet in your shoes.
You can steer yourself in
any direction you choose.
You're on your own.
And you know what you know.
You are the guy who'll decide
where to go."
—Dr. Seuss

TOP TEN THINGS EVERY GRADUATE SHOULD KNOW

10

Kim Foster

EDITOR, FRIEND, WIFE TO AWARD WINNING TEACHER CHUCK FOSTER

1. Explore as many career options as possible. Don't limit yourself to one line of thinking. Today's world honors diversity and flexibility in skills and experience.

2. Find worthy mentors who demonstrate integrity and have mastered their craft. Learn as much as you can from experts you admire.

3. Take advantage of any testing that will help determine your strengths and interests and where those intersect. You may be surprised at what you learn.

4. Learn the strengths and weaknesses of your personality. The knowledge will give you clarity when choosing a vocation.

5. Balance your checkbook. Don't guess at what's in your account. Cross your t's and dot your i's financially. Leave the guesswork to Wall Street.

6. Write a budget. If you're relying on a set amount of income, you need to know how to divvy it up.

7. Learn to live affordably. Don't get sucked into credit card debt. It's a deep hole and hard to get out of. Live within your means.

8. Be willing to endure delayed gratification. Drive the affordable car that works well but isn't the latest model. If it runs and gets decent gas mileage, be thankful.

9. Take deadlines seriously. Learn to budget your time. Employers and clients are not always forgiving of tardiness.

10. Live without regrets. Think through choices you make and the consequences, whether positive or negative. These decisions will follow you throughout your life.

Kim Foster is a local editor with experience in editing nonfiction books (self-help, inspirational, leadership, business, health, and religious), graduate-level theses, and doctoral dissertations. She has been the primary editor of several award-winning books. Kim lives in the Treasure Valley with her husband, and together they search for books that will no longer fit on any shelf.

Terry Heffner

DAD, FORMER STUDENT-ATHLETE AT BOISE STATE UNIVERSITY, BUSINESS OWNER, LIFE DIRECTOR WITH BUILDING CONTRACTORS ASSOCIATION

1. Read books regularly.

2. Strive to be the best version of yourself every day.

3. Focus less on your personal achievements. Serve others and you will achieve your goals.

4. Tomorrow was never promised; live every day as if it's your last.

5. Always let your Mom and Dad know you love them, and tell them as often as you can.

6. Be sure to tell your friends you love them; no one ever makes it alone.

7. Love your brothers and sisters no matter what; families are forever.

8. Do not wish your life away, live in the moment.

9. Be open to new relationships, do not limit yourself to few or, worse yet, to one person.

10. When looking for solutions, do more of what works, less of what does not.

Terry Heffner is a native Idahoan. He graduated from Boise State University with a BAA in Business and was a four year letterman in football. He is a life director with the Building Contractors Association and a member of the Bishop Kelly Foundation Board. He is very active in the local community organizations and events as well as coaching youth in all sports.

TOP TEN THINGS EVERY GRADUATE SHOULD KNOW

10

Kurt Koontz

AUTHOR, SPEAKER, TRAVELER, RECREATIONAL ELITE ATHLETE

1. Take a yearlong solo journey to a foreign country before entering college.

2. Eat healthier food.

3. The drama portion of your life is now behind you. Let it go and never reengage.

4. Exercise for one hour at least five times per week.

5. Take a class on meditation and incorporate yoga into your life.

6. Make a diverse list of five things you have never done. Do them over the next year and make a new list.

7. Volunteer in your community.

8. Thank your parents for putting up with your crap. You never fooled them.

9. Date a musician or artist.

10. Follow the two ears and one mouth rule until death.

After retiring early from his job as a successful sales executive for a Fortune 500 technology company, Kurt Koontz volunteered in his community and traveled across Europe and North America. He never considered writing a book until he walked nearly 500 miles across Spain in 2012. Those million steps were so compelling that he returned home and began writing and speaking about his life-changing adventures. He lives and writes on a tree-lined creek in Boise, Idaho.

Matt Payn

MENTOR, DAD OF TWO SONS,
ACCOUNT EXECUTIVE WITH
GLOBAL ENERGY & LIGHTING

1. Recognize life is precious.

   I've lost at least two high school classmates since I graduated, one to renal failure and the other to the "weight loss" drug Ephedra before it was banned. Death ushers in a greater perspective of reality. Life is too short and you realize who you missed and how you fell short when someone is gone.

   Appreciate the people around you. Let me pause to be very clear. Not just those you care about. Everyone's life is precious, yet too often I found myself pretending like some people were important and others didn't matter. I wish I had been more intentional about caring for all of the people around me.

2. Remember your life is precious.

   Too often we consider everyone else at risk of death, and ourselves invincible. I never thought about the possibility that my own life could be cut short. Your life span is undetermined. How sad it is when we make decisions that risk our own lives, and sadder still when someone else makes a decision that takes another life. If you hold onto the perspective that your life is precious, you'll avoid making decisions that risk cutting yours short.

(3.)   Realize the world doesn't revolve around you.

It was so easy to be ensnared by the trap that the world revolved around me. I was having fun, doing well in school and focusing on college. I met my future wife as a senior; however, as I look back on my high school years I can't think of a single thing I did that was truly important.

Had I died when I was nineteen, people would have said "he was such a nice young man," but that's it. The only person I was truly focused on was me and subsequently I had no profound impact on the lives of the people around me. Commit to spending time each day focused on how to impact others in a positive way.

(4.)   You can make a difference.

Often times I considered really big accomplishments to be success. My attitude, especially years ago was that something important meant impacting hundreds of thousands or millions of people.

If this is you, let me give you a reality check. It doesn't take monumental effort to make an impact that leaves a lasting impression. Making a difference can be as simple as making a positive impact on one person. Amazingly, if you make a difference in the life of one person per week starting at the age of sixteen, you will influence 3,640 people by 86 years of age.

5. Your siblings can be your best friends.

My first memory of my brother is about four or five years old. I probably stopped being friends with my younger brother when I was sixteen. Doing the quick math, that is eleven or twelve years of friendship with my brother that I missed. I've now been living in a different town and only seeing my younger brother periodically (one to three times per year) for the last eighteen years. The only siblings you'll ever have in your life are the ones you've been given.

In my life, I'm thankful that our friendship began growing again in our mid 20's. I consider my brother a true friend now, but I missed an opportunity and can never get those years back.

6. Find confidence in being yourself.

You were made unique. You are here for a purpose (whether you're walking towards or in that purpose or not). Being yourself is founded in having confidence in the gifts, skills, and personality characteristics that you have been given.

7. Don't wear a mask.

Wearing a mask and being yourself are similar but unique enough to be separate concepts. High school is full of masks. Although I didn't wear a mask often in high school, it's an incredibly pervasive issue.

It's ok to have real problems. You don't have to hide everything from those you trust. Vulnerability isn't something to be ashamed of. In fact, hiding problems makes them much worse. Bring to light the areas that feed and grow in the darkness.

8.   Embrace mistakes.

The most successful entrepreneurs and business people have pushed through the mistakes they've made to improve their product, idea, or focus. Mistakes are learning experiences if you allow them to be. Be willing to give yourself grace when you make a mistake. Just learn from it.

9.   Give your best.

The difference between success and failure is your effort. I didn't give my best often in my high school years or early adult life. Now I realize that even if the outcome of a situation is a failure, it counts as a success if I put forth my best effort.

10. Realize you are responsible for the outcome of your life.

Matt Payn has a gift and passion for people and building relationships. With a diverse background and MBA, he works in the entrepreneurial business environment and applies his relationship building talent along with aptitude for many areas of business to excel. He prioritizes his life as faith, family, work, friends and community (coaching youth baseball, neighborhood involvement, church, mentoring young people).

TOP TEN THINGS EVERY GRADUATE SHOULD KNOW 10

Tobe Brockner

ENTREPRENEUR, AUTHOR, CONSULTANT, SPEAKER

1. Talent is overrated. Never underestimate the power of just outworking the other person. Intelligence, talent, and know-how are almost always trumped by grit.

2. Focus on purpose first, profits second. Money is important, but it's not everything. Concentrate on making a dent in the universe and the money will follow.

3. Lead by example. The very best way to lead others is to serve as an example of someone to aspire to. The best leaders are the best because others want to emulate them. Be that person.

4. Don't worry so much about what society expects from you. Live your own life on your own terms.

5. Always live the Platinum Rule: Do unto others as they would have you do unto them.

6. Pay things forward. Pay it forward even when you think you can't. Pay it forward even if you think it will never come back to you. Pay it forward even to those you don't think deserve it.

7. Keep a wary eye on debt and spending. Learn to delay instant gratification.

8. Focus, focus, focus. Distraction is the enemy of success.

9. There are three keys to long term happiness in your life. Find something you love to do that you're also good at, and something for which you can be paid well.

10. Above all else, never stop learning. High school graduation is called "commencement" for a reason: your life has just begun.

Tobe Brockner has been an entrepreneur his whole life, starting his first business as a baseball trading-card broker in the second grade. After graduating from Boise State University, he started marketing and advertising business that serves small business owners and teaches them how to market their products and services better. As a result of these relationships, Tobe has created and runs several local Mastermind Groups. In his free time, Tobe enjoys reading, writing, and spending time with his wife, Kirsten, and their two children, Beau and Scarlett.

Scott & Maribel Morrell

DENTISTS AND PROUD PARENTS

1. Do what you love. Doing something you don't like is exhausting and will not produce long term success. Doing things you love *gives* you energy. Doing things you dislike *exhausts* your energy. Find things in life you really enjoy and pursue those.

2. Make everyone around you feel appreciated and validated. Be willing to help others at every opportunity. People won't always remember what you do for them, but they will remember *how you make them feel*.

3. Don't take rejection or bad behavior personally. If you are doing the right thing and working earnestly to the best you can, understand that someone's bad behavior toward you is not about *you,* it is about *them*. So take these episodes as the bumps in the road that they are, and don't internalize them. Never let them impact the direction in your life or how you feel about yourself.

4. You *are* smart enough. If you are not #1 in your class, don't despair. More than half of the richest, most suc-

cessful people in the country didn't even finish college. Supreme academic achievement is nice, but it is by no means a free pass to success. You have to be *smart enough* to be successful, and the good news is that almost everyone is. So are you.

5.) Tenacity is the key to success. Great ideas and class valedictorians are a dime a dozen. The difference between those who succeed and those who don't is pure grit, determination, and the willingness to overcome obstacles. Understand this, and build tenacity into the foundation of who you are.

6.) Learn to finish. They say starting is the hardest part. Not true. Finishing is the hardest. Those who are successful have learned to not leave great ideas on the workbench, but to execute and follow through with relentless determination to *finish* the idea at all costs. Most often, you will gain confidence in finishing strong — in everything you do.

7.) Learn to care about details. Success is about doing lots of little things well. Whether you are a laborer or a neurosurgeon, doing a job successfully depends on your ability to focus on and master the little things that others cannot do in regard to the task at hand. You will differentiate yourself in life and in your career by learning to proficiently execute the little things.

8.) Learn to make good decisions. If you constantly make poor choices you will end up being your own worst enemy. Do what is right — even when it's hard. When confronted by a dilemma, take the more challenging, difficult moral path.

9. Be decisive. You will never have perfect, complete information with which to make most decisions in life. So gather all the appropriate information that you can, and thoughtfully consider your options — then make the decision and do it! Endlessly analyzing can paralyze you, make you unable to move forward and will limit your growth.

10. Get rid of social insecurities. If someone doesn't talk to you, don't assume they think they are better than you, or dislike you. It's usually not true. In most cases others are just as socially insecure as you are, or even more so.

W. Scott Morrell & Maribel C. Morrell, are both graduates of the University of Iowa College of Dentistry, and have been in the clinical practice of dentistry for more than 24 years. Both enjoy traveling, good food, skiing, cycling, and entertaining their many wonderful friends. They are the proud parents of Ashley and James Morrell.

James—We are so proud of you for being the young man you are. Your decision to share all you have learned with others, and make a difference in the lives of others will create a legacy of which you can be very proud.

—Mom and Dad

Conclusion

You have now seen great advice from some very outstanding people. Now what? I strongly encourage you to take this to heart, as I have, and begin using it in your daily life. Hundreds of times during my youth, my mother has reminded me to not "reinvent the wheel," but rather learn from the experience and actions of others. We can truly exceed the success of others by applying these values to our own lives and taking action with the wisdom we have received.

It takes about three weeks of repeatedly doing an action to form a new habit. If you are to be successful and allow this information to make a real difference in your life, then I would suggest you do what I am doing: Take two or three items that really mean something to you and write them down somewhere you will see them everyday. Review them daily, without fail, preferably in the morning. Read them, say them out loud, think on them, and try to internalize the message each day for several weeks. In this way, you will maximize the wisdom of this material and enable it to make a substantial impact in your life.

Some of my favorite pieces of advice that I am working on now are:

1. Doing my best to be the "go-to" guy who is reliable and can get the job done.

2. Educating myself about money, and learning to be responsible with it which will pave the way to a better financial future.

3. Stop worrying about the "what if" scenarios and learn to enjoy everyone and everything in life each day. Additionally I am setting intentional goals around much more of the advice in this book. I trust you will do the same.

4. Ensuring that I advance on to college, determined to succeed, and not view it as a way to delay adulthood for a few more years. I am going to take advantage of as many opportunities as I can and gain experiences which will help me out in the long run.

The lessons you have learned in this book will give you clarity and direction as well as confidence in making good decisions for what lies ahead. You will have many successful days and lots of challenging ones. In the midst of the good and bad, I encourage you to review the advice of from this book and your own list to remind yourself what you have chosen to value and prioritize. Don't forget to see the best in yourself and the people around you on your epic journey.

Top Ten Most Important Things to Remember

1. _____

2. _____

3. _____

4. _____

5. _____

6. _____

7. _____

8. _____

9. _____

10. _____

Notes

TOP TEN THINGS EVERY
GRADUATE SHOULD KNOW

10

Notes

Notes

Acknowledgments

Writing a book is a very daunting and challenging task that requires a large devotion of time, effort, and patience. There are quite a few people that I owe a big thanks to for helping me put this book together.

First off, I want to say thank you to all of my contributors who helped put this book together. I really appreciate each of you taking the time to create thoughtful and unique lists. Each of you has provided an interesting perspective and I hope that we can all work together again in the future.

I would also like to thank Maryanna Young, Hannah Cross, and the rest of the Aloha staff who guided, assisted, and coached me through this process. It has been a real pleasure to work with all of you and I am looking forward to the next project we pursue.

To my grandmother and grandfather: thank you for bringing constant support and care into my life. I have learned so many valuable lessons from each of you and will carry them into my life as I continue to grow and gain more experiences.

To my sister Ashley: thank you for always motivating me to be better. I have looked up to you since we were children and I want to thank you for being the sister that you are. Your guidance has enabled me to discover my potential in life and I know I will be more successful in my future because of the knowledge I have gained from you.

Mom and Papa: your leadership and guidance has kept me motivated, focused, and on task. Thank you for your patience and for all of the time that you devoted to helping me write this book. You have always inspired me to be hard working and passionate about everything that I do. Your lessons have instilled confidence in me and I know that I will move on, driven to pursue bigger and better things in my future. Thank you for helping me develop an intense work ethic and a positive outlook on life. I love you guys.

I could not have made this book happen without the support of each and every one of you and I cannot wait till the next.

Regards,

James Michael Morrell

About the Author

Since middle school, James Michael Morrell has been devoted to fitness, athletics, and having a positive influence on those around him. Always open to new opportunities and willing to challenge his comfort zone, James involved himself in a wide variety of activities. During his high school years, he continued to be involved in his primary love: football. In addition he was a varsity wrestler, swimmer, and water polo player as well as a participant in numerous triathlons and the NGA Idaho Bodybuilding Championships.

Aside from his fondness for athletics and fitness, James has pursued activities that put him in positions of leadership. His student Government experience includes Student Body President of SJMS and ASB Secretary of Bishop Kelly High School. He was also elected as a team captain for the BK swim team during his junior school year. James loves speaking to groups about personal development and character growth, and has spent time helping younger students prepare themselves for their future endeavors.

Work experiences include starting his own athletic video productions business, including the production of a full-length documentary on Bishop Kelly's 2013 State Championship Football Season. He has also worked as a lifeguard, swim instructor, and a car detailer in his hometown of Boise, Idaho. His next task is to discover his future potential as an author.

James has served his community in a variety of ways, including work at the Idaho Botanical Gardens, the Boise Gun club, and as a youth coach and referee at various athletic tournaments and camps. Additionally, Campus Ministry work and altar serving at his local church have played an important role in helping James grow spiritually.

His latest challenge is to assemble a practical guide to personal development for his peers. His passion for the subject motivated him to contact people from various walks of life to gain insights into their perspectives on success. The outgrowth of this pursuit is the work, *Epic Advice for Graduates*.

James' ultimate goal is to find personal satisfaction through his work. He believes that adhering to the highest standards of integrity, respectability, and ethics in his work will allow him to aid others in finding their potential and enhance their future experiences. Lifelong learning is also important to him in order to promote growth – both personal and professional. He hopes to continue growing intellectually so that he may lead others to a path that allows for optimal growth in their futures.

More About
The Epic Book Series

In the coming months and years, more Epic books are set to be written based on what individuals, organizations, schools, universities and corporations request for their audiences.

Additional Books in the Epic Series

- *Epic Advice As You Head to College: Key Reminders to Change the Entire Experience*
- *Epic Advice on Simple Dieting for First Time Bodybuilders*
- *Epic Advice for Maximum Performance for High School Athletes*
- *Epic Advice to Stop Bullying In Your School*

If you have ideas for additional Epic book series books, please send us a note at AlohaPublishing.com or email us at alohapublishing@gmail.com. We'll pass your comments on to the author, James Morrell.

Do You Want to Buy
a Large Quantity of
Epic Advice for Graduates Books?

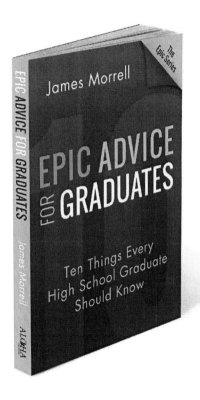

Please call Aloha Publishing at
(208) 447-9036
Send us a text message or email us
alohapublishing@gmail.com
Huge discounts for quantities of 10 to 10,000.